DELETE

D1539085

SandCastle 3

Good Manners

May I?

Kelly Doudna

ABDO
Publishing Company

FX: 4/16

Published by SandCastle™, an imprint of ABDO Publishing Company, 4940 Viking Drive, Edina, Minnesota 55435.

Printed in the United States.

Cover and interior photo credits: Eyewire Images, Digital Stock, Stock Market

Library of Congress Cataloging-in-Publication Data

Doudna, Kelly, 1963-
    May I? / Kelly Doudna.
        p. cm. -- (Good manners)
    Includes index.
    ISBN 1-57765-572-9
        1. Courtesy--Juvenile literature. 2. Children--Conduct of life. 3. Etiquette. [1. Etiquette.] I. Title.

BJ1533.C9 D686 2001
395.1'22--dc21

                                                                    2001022000

The SandCastle concept, content, and reading method have been reviewed and approved by a national advisory board including literacy specialists, librarians, elementary school teachers, early childhood education professionals, and parents.

Let Us Know

After reading the book, SandCastle would like you to tell us your stories about reading. What is your favorite page? Was there something hard that you needed help with? Share the ups and downs of learning to read. We want to hear from you! To get posted on the ABDO Publishing Company Web site, send us email at:

sandcastle@abdopub.com

About SandCastle™
Nonfiction books for the beginning reader

- Basic concepts of phonics are incorporated with integrated language methods of reading instruction. Most words are short, and phrases, letter sounds, and word sounds are repeated.

- Readability is determined by the number of words in each sentence, the number of characters in each word, and word lists based on curriculum frameworks.

- Full-color photography reinforces word meanings and concepts.

- "Words I Can Read" list at the end of each book teaches basic elements of grammar, helps the reader recognize the words in the text, and builds vocabulary.

- Reading levels are indicated by the number of flags on the castle.

Look for more SandCastle books in these three reading levels:

Level 1 (one flag)	**Level 2** (two flags)	**Level 3** (three flags)

Grades Pre-K to K 5 or fewer words per page	**Grades K to 1** 5 to 10 words per page	**Grades 1 to 2** 10 to 15 words per page

We say "**may I**" when we ask to do or have something.

We often say **"may I"** and "please" together.

This shows that we have good manners.

Selma eats a salad for lunch.

She asks, "**May I** have a napkin please?"

Polly plays a game.

She asks, "**May I** have more time for my turn?"

Walt watches while his brother and grandfather play chess.

He asks, "**May I** play next?"

Pam plays on the swing.

Her brother asks, "**May I** have a turn please?"

Wes decides he would rather walk next to his brother.

He asks, "**May I** get down?"

Marcy is at the park with her mom.

She asks, "**May I** feed the geese?"

When Bob finishes his book, Winnie would like to read it.

How should she ask?

Words I Can Read

Nouns

A noun is a person, place, or thing

book (BUK) p. 21
brother (BRUHTH-ur) pp. 13, 15, 17
chess (CHESS) p. 13
game (GAME) p. 11

grandfather (GRAND-fah-thur) p. 13
lunch (LUHNCH) p. 9
mom (MOM) p. 19
napkin (NAP-kin) p. 9

park (PARK) p. 19
salad (SAL-uhd) p. 9
swing (SWING) p. 15
time (TIME) p. 11
turn (TURN) pp. 11, 15

Proper Nouns

A proper noun is the name of a person, place, or thing

Bob (BOB) p. 21
Marcy (MAR-see) p. 19
Pam (PAM) p. 15

Polly (POL-ee) p. 11
Selma (SEL-muh) p. 9
Walt (WAWLT) p. 13

Wes (WESS) p. 17
Winnie (WIN-ee) p. 21

Plural Nouns

A plural noun is more than one person, place, or thing

geese (GEESS) p. 19
manners (MAN-urz) p. 7

Pronouns

A pronoun is a word that replaces a noun

he (HEE) pp. 13, 17
I (EYE) pp. 5, 7, 9, 11, 13, 15, 17, 19
it (IT) p. 21

something (SUHM-thing) p. 5
she (SHEE) pp. 9, 11, 19, 21

this (THISS) p. 7
we (WEE) pp. 5, 7

Verbs

A verb is an action or being word

ask (ASK) pp. 5, 21
asks (ASKSS) pp. 9, 11, 13, 15, 17, 19
decides (di-SIDEZ) p. 17
do (DOO) p. 5
eats (EETSS) p. 9
feed (FEED) p. 19
finishes (FIN-ish-iz) p. 21
get (GET) p. 17

have (HAV) pp. 5, 7, 9, 11, 15
is (IZ) p. 19
like (LIKE) p. 21
may (MAY) pp. 5, 7, 9, 11, 13, 15, 17, 19
play (PLAY) p. 13
plays (PLAYZ) p. 15
read (REED) p. 21

say (SAY) pp. 5, 7
should (SHUD) p. 21
shows (SHOHZ) p. 7
walk (WAWK) p. 17
watches (WOCH-iz) p. 13
would (WUD) pp. 17, 21

Adjectives

An adjective describes something

good (GUD) p. 7
her (HUR) pp. 15, 19

his (HIZ) pp. 13, 17, 21
more (MOR) p. 11

my (MYE) p. 11
next (NEKST) p. 17

Adverbs

An adverb tells how, when, or where something happens

down (DOUN) p. 17
how (HOU) p. 21
next (NEKST) p. 13

often (OF-uhn) p. 7
please (PLEEZ) pp. 7, 9, 15

rather (RA-thur) p. 17
together (tuh-GETH-ur) p. 7

23

Glossary

chess – a game for two people with 16 pieces each, played on a board marked with squares of alternating colors.

geese – large birds with long necks and webbed feet.

manners – polite behavior.

napkin – a square piece of paper or cloth used to protect the clothes while eating and to wipe hands and lips.

salad – a mixture of raw vegetables usually served with a dressing.